Herbert Karner, Artur Rosenauer and Werner Telesko

THE AUSTRIAN ACADEMY OF SCIENCES

THE BUILDING AND ITS HISTORY

Austrian Academy
of Sciences Press

Vienna 2007

ÖAW

Vorgelegt von w. M. Artur Rosenauer
in der Sitzung am 23. März 2007

Die verwendete Papiersorte ist aus
chlorfrei gebleichtem Zellstoff hergestellt,
frei von säurebildenden Bestandteilen
und alterungsbeständig.

British Library Cataloguing in Publication Data.
A Catalogue record of this book is available
from the British Library.

Photo Cover: ÖAW;
Academy of Fine Arts, Vienna

Translated by Mag. Eva Beckel, Vienna

ISBN 978-3-7001-3876-1
Copyright © 2007 by Österreichische
Akademie der Wissenschaften
Wien

Printed and bound in Austria by:
Grasl Druck & Neue Medien,
A-2540 Bad Vöslau;
Design: Elke Salzer, www.info@diegrafikerin.at

http://hw.oeaw.ac.at/3876-1
http:verlag.oeaw.ac.at

Table of contents

Foreword

The present guide is to give the interested public an idea of the structural features and interior decoration of the building which was erected in 1755 as the Aula of the University of Vienna and has accommodated the Academy of Sciences since 1857.

This publication owes its existence first and foremost to my colleagues Dr. Herbert Karner and Univ.-Doz. Dr. Werner Telesko. They have been kind enough to include my name in the list of authors even though my share is limited to contributions on the work of Franz Anton Maulbertsch and editorial activities.

In the interest of readability we have refrained from discussing in detail a number of recent research findings, which we hope will be made available to the scientific world in a separate, more detailed publication.

I should like to thank the Verlag der Österreichischen Akademie der Wissenschaften for their valuable support and the attractive design of this publication.

Artur Rosenauer, Ordinary Member
Chairman, Commission for the History of Art of the Austrian Academy of Sciences

The antecedents of the New University Aula:
"Collegium Ducale" and "Unteres Jesuiterplatzl"

The building, which has accommodated the Austrian Academy of Sciences since 1857, was built as the "New Aula" of the University of Vienna under the Empress Maria Theresa. The choice of the building site was deliberate, since it was located in the quarter that had been home to the university since the late 14th century. It is not exactly known what buildings had initially been available to the University of Vienna when it was founded in 1365. In 1384 Duke Albrecht III founded the "Collegium Ducale", which was accommodated in a group of buildings between the "Prediger" ("Preachers"), the Dominican Monastery, and what was then Filzerstrasse (an extension of what is today Riemergasse), approximately in the place of today's eastern wing of the Jesuit College at Postgasse 5–9 (**Fig. 1**).

In the 15th century the complex was extended to the south and west, in the area of the junction of Filzerstrasse with Vordere Bäckerstrasse (now Bäckerstrasse), Hintere Bäckerstrasse (now Sonnenfelsgasse) and the short Schulgasse lane, by the addition of the Faculty of Arts building called "Structura nova" or "Neue Schul" and the "Libreye" (library). These central buildings of the university were

surrounded by a number of detached buildings, the so-called "bursae" (student lodgings) such as the Sprenger, Lamm and Bruck bursae, the open and irregular structure of which remained typical of the university quarter well into the 17th century. Bonifaz Wolmuet's Map of Vienna of 1547 (**Fig. 2**) designates the buildings as "Der universitet Collegium", "Aula universitatis" and "Librey".

Major changes were made in 1622 when the Emperor Ferdinand II entrusted the completely derelict Faculty of Arts and the Faculty of Theology to the Jesuits, who had been called to Vienna by his grandfather, King Ferdinand I, in the course of the Counter-Reformation. This meant that the Jesuits were responsible for 95 per cent of the Viennese students. Accordingly, room had to be made in the densely built-up

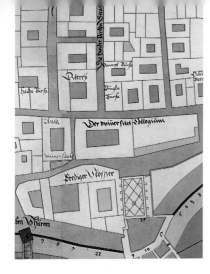

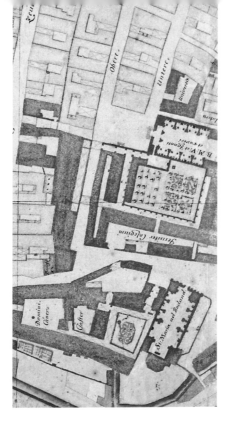

B. WOLMUET,
MAP OF VIENNA,
1547 (DETAIL
UNIVERSITY
QUARTER)
(FIG. 2)

W. A. STEINHAUSEN,
MAP OF VIENNA,
1710 (DETAIL
UNIVERSITY
QUARTER)
(FIG. 3)

AERIAL PHOTO-
GRAPH OF
UNIVERSITY
QUARTER
(FIG. 4)

university quarter for a Jesuit college. Vienna was the centre of the vast Austrian province of the Order, which extended from Passau to Hermannstadt (now Sibiu) and from Vienna to Belgrade. A radical solution with far-reaching consequences in terms of town planning was necessary to demonstrate the predominant position of the Jesuits and to meet the triple space requirements for a church, school and lodgings, as evidenced by a comparison of Wohlmuet's Map of Vienna and the one of Werner Arnold Steinhausen from the year 1710 (**Fig. 3**).

The part of Riemergasse immediately after its intersection with Wollzeile was sacrificed so that the street would abut with the free-standing school wing today called the "Old Aula" (to distinguish it from Maria Theresa's "New Aula"). The building, with its still extant huge Jesuit theatre, was connected with the massive main buildings grouped around a central courtyard by raised structures bridging the extension of Bäckerstrasse. In order to make room for the northward extension of the three-winged main building and the dominant church next to it, the neighbouring area had first to be razed. The necessary space was obtained by clearing Schulstrasse, Filzerstrasse and part of Hintere Bäcker-strasse and dismantling old structures, in particular the "Collegium Ducale" and other university buildings such as the library and the Lamm bursa (**Fig. 4**).

Room for a church square was made by razing the two plots in front. This square, called "Unteres Jesuiterplatzl", was to enhance the architectural effect of the church façade and at the same time provide the university quarter with a new centre giving access to both the church and the university, the "Collegium Academicum Viennense". Salomon Kleiner's copper engraving of 1724 (**Fig. 5**) illustrates this new concept. The Early Baroque church façade with its sculptures and monumental inscription proclaims the programmatic message of the Counter-Reformation. Its urbanistic function as the central element of the ensemble is accentuated by the noble reticence of the lateral façades of the square: on the right-hand, eastern flank the College, on the left, western side a two-storeyed building still known as "Schwaigerburse" in the 16th century. Since the building adjoining its eastern flank was razed in 1624 when the square was created, the façade of the "Schwaigerburse" was by and large designed on the model of the College on the opposite side. According to Salomon Kleiner's engraving of 1724 it belonged at that time to Count Collalto.

Maria Theresa's plans for a new university building

Ever since 1752 Maria Theresa had planned to give the university, which suffered from a deplorable lack of space, more dignified premises. On 26 February 1753 she gave orders to "[...] find a suitable location for a university building to be erected, affording sufficient residences for all professores Juris and Medicinae, but first and foremost providing the juridical and medical faculties with the required rooms and halls for their lectures and actibus publicis as well as other requirements [...]". In a lengthy submission on 15 March 1753 to the Empress, the "Directorium in publicis et cameralibus" – formed in 1749 in the course of Maria Theresa's administrative reforms by the merger of all but two departments of the "Hofkammer" with the "Hofkanzlei" – for the first time described in detail the requirements regarding the construction, uses and equipment of a university building. The original idea to provide residential quarters for all professors of the juridical and medical faculties was mainly due to the wish to give preferential treatment to the faculties most affected by the university reform. Ultimately it was, however, decided that the new university building should accommodate all four faculties even if this meant that not all space requirements could be met.

By February 1754 the decision to accommodate the four faculties in one new building had become the official policy, stressing the inseparability of all academic disciplines – a point of view that is convincingly reflected in the first sketches for the frescoes that were to decorate the Great Hall (and which had already been anticipated in the programme for Anton Hertzog's fresco for the library of the Jesuit College [around 1735] [**Fig. 6**]). The new university building can be considered to be representative of Maria Theresa's energetic reorganisation of academic life, which aimed at giving the sciences, with their increasingly rational basis, a more practical orientation. The sciences "serving the public good" (Friederich Colland) thus gained greater significance among the academic disciplines.

The new building and the topographical situation of the University Square

In order to make room for the new university building other buildings had to be razed: the one at the western flank of Jesuitenplatz as well as two other buildings behind it. There seemed to be a tacit agreement that the original function of the square as the centre of the university quarters was not to be changed (see Fig. 3). This urbanistic sine qua non and the narrow space available required an unusual design of the "New Aula". The narrow front facing the square had to be accentuated by the design of the main façade. This new façade was to compete directly with the front of the church, which had so far dominated the square, so that the square was put into a new visual perspective (Fig. 7). The attenuation of the predominance of the church by the new university building symbolises the reorganisation of university teaching, in the course of which – as regards the disciplines of theology and philosophy – the "Societas Jesu" was to be gradually deprived of its influence by 1759.

The originally intended design of the square appears to have been much more radical than the actual outcome. Still existing drawings caused Renate Wagner-Rieger to speak about plans for a veritable "university forum". An elevation of the Jesuit College opposite the new building dating from the years after 1773 indicates that it was planned to heighten the College façade by two further five-bay storeys at the centre and to top them with a "Mathematical Tower".

The building on the fourth side of the square opposite the church was also to accommodate parts of the university. The building was owned by Conrad Adolph von Albrecht (who died in 1751), the famous concettista of Emperor Charles VI, who ranks prominently in the cultural history of the Viennese Baroque era as the author of the iconographic programme for the decorations of St. Charles's Church and the Court Library. The Archbishop of Vienna, Johann Joseph Graf von Trautson (1704–1757), (Prince-Archbishop of Vienna 1751–1757) and Protector of the University, intended to include the building in the university complex and adapt it as residential building for the professors. The idea was only dropped at the end of 1753, months after construction of the university building had started.

As far as we can see from still existing documents and pictures, it was planned not only to erect a single university building but to implement a large-scale project to redefine this part of the town,

which had been used for university purposes since the Middle Ages, in urbanistic terms and give it a clear architectural structure. This project from the years around 1750 got stuck halfway – but at least the central new university building, an architectural masterpiece, has been realised.

Publications on the occasion of the official inauguration of the new university building

The new university building was not big enough to meet all academic needs, and the university therefore continued to use other locations, as it had done in some way or other for a long time. In Maria Theresa's concept, Jean Nicolas de Jadot's new building was seen to form the "principal university building" (Justus Schmidt) and the ideational centre of all the other decentralised locations. The Empress not only intended the old buildings to continue to be used by the university but at the same time sought to acquire other buildings in the vicinity to accommodate lodgings for the teachers as well as lecture halls.

Construction of the building was completed in the summer of 1755 and the official inauguration took place on 5 April 1756. Kneeling before the Empress, the President of the Directorate, Friedrich Wilhelm Graf Haugwitz (1702–1765), received the keys of the university from her hands and passed them on to the University Protector Archbishop Johann Josef Graf von Trautson, who handed them over to the Rector Magnificus, Regierungsrat Johann Adam von Penz.

A number of informative publications appeared on the occasion of the inauguration of the new university building, such as the festschrift edited by the epicist and art theoretician Franz Christoph Scheyb (also known as Orestrio) (1704–1777) entitled "Musae Francisco et Mariae Theresiae Augustis congratulantur ob scientias bonasque artes eorum iussu et munificentia Vindobonae restitutas" (Vienna 1756). This interesting publication, which begins with the age of the Babenberg Duke Heinrich II. Jasomirgott, constitutes an apotheosis of the reigning couple Franz I Stephan and Maria Theresa. It sings the praise of the Habsburg rulers as generous patrons of the arts and the sciences. "[...] Ye are the couple the muse sang of,.. [...]". This panegyric was not the only one to be published on the occasion: In the same year, Scheyb composed "Heinrich Jasomirgott – eine Lobschrift auf Ihre Kaiserliche und Koenigliche Majestaeten bey Gelegenheit der uralten Universität zu Wien von dem Arkader Orestrio" ("Heinrich Jasomirgott – a panegyric on their Imperial and Royal Majesties on the occasion of the Old University of Vienna by the Arcadian Orestrio" [Vienna 1756]). In this work, the activities of the Imperial couple are seen as the culmination of the century-old munificent patronage of the Babenbergs and Habsburgs: "[...] A pair that brings peace and wards off misery, the rulers of all hearts that only the vicious fear, whose rule is rich in love, compassion and mercy [...]".

The glorification of the Habsburgs culminated in the 47-page "Panegyricus Francisco et Mariae Theresiae Augustis ob scientias optimasque artes suis in terris instauratas, ornatas (...)" (Vienna 1756) written by the Viennese Jesuit and Professor of Rhetoric Georg Maister, which was also

Ioannes Iosephus a Trautshon Archiepiscopus Viennensis in Austria, Viennensis S.R.E. Presbyter Cardinalis creatus á SSmo D.N. BENEDICTO XIV in Consistorio secreto die 5 Aprilis 1756. Obijt die 10 Martij 1757.
I.A. Faldoni sculp.

published in a French version. In contains a verbose description of how the sciences have now moved from humble and miserable buildings to a new regal palace ("novum regale palatium") and how the previously neglected academic disciplines are now imbued with new life. Since the new building was dedicated to all faculties, it is even called a "castle of common felicity" ("arcem communis felicitatis"), as "Austria's hope" ("spem Austriae") and as "Germany's jewel" ("decus Germaniae"). The panegyric reaches its climax in the praise of Jadot's architectural creation and calls it a "firmament of peace, religion, justice and universal weal" ("firmamentum pacis, religionis, justitiae, salutis universorum"). The commitment of the Imperial couple to the sciences is exuberantly praised as "paternal solicitude" ("Paterna Solicitudine [sic!]") and "maternal clemency" ("Materna Clementia"). The document does not contain any relevant comments on the building as such and mentions only the group of statues

in the Great Hall as allegories of the arts, the sciences and virtues.

The glorification of the generous patronage of the Imperial couple as the central message of Gregorio Guglielmi's ceiling fresco in the Great Hall (1755) was thus the central issue of all the panegyrics published on the occasion of the inauguration of the new university building. Like Guglielmi's fresco, the authors do not focus on the broad spectrum of intellectual activities of the university but rather on the Imperial patrons, who claimed to usher in a "Golden Age" of scholarship and science. It is in this spirit that the "Ode à leurs majestés imperiales et roïales à l'occasion du rétablissement de l'université de Vienne (Vienna–Prague 1756) have to be read, which – in connection with Jadot's new building – sees the advent of an "heureux siècle de Titus" and a "beau siècle d'Auguste", the glorious ages in Roman antiquity under the Emperors Augustus and Titus. Franz I Stephan and Maria Theresa were also honoured as patrons of the sciences on a medal designed by Matthäus Donner (featuring the façade of the new university building and the circumscription "MUNIFICENTIA AUGUSTORUM." [1756]), which was distributed on the occasion of the inauguration of the new building.

History of planning, construction and functions

The driving force behind the speedy realisation of the construction was the Protector of the University of Vienna, Archbishop Johann Joseph Graf Trautson (**Fig. 8**), whom Empress Maria Theresa had entrusted with the overall responsibility for all matters of construction in March 1753, at a point in time when all planning activities were already in full swing. The court had been in possession of rough drafts of the design and appearance of the building and known the name of the architect to be commissioned to implement it already since the beginning of the year. A submission to the Empress of 15 February 1753 reads: "[...] likewise there will be need for four entrances to the building so that carriages can enter on one side and leave on the other, since no large courtyards will be feasible. To ascertain in what way everything can be done properly it will be necessary to have preliminary plans and elevations drawn and, as Your Imperial Royal Majesty has already deigned to demand that the new building be constructed with graceful façade on all four sides and especially on the side of the square in front of the Jesuit Church, for which purpose Court Building Inspector de Jadot is to design the necessary elevations. It will therefore be Your Majesty's decision whether de Jadot is to be ordered to produce such elevations, and to graciously determine who is to prepare the other elevations, plans and material requirements and thus be in charge of the erection of the building. [...]"

It is fairly unusual that at a time when no definitive plans existed about the structure and the layout of the rooms, Jean Nicolas de Jadot had already been designated as the architect responsible for the façades. According to the above source it remained to be decided who was to draw up all the other plans and be responsible for the management of construction. This explains why there is a certain inconsistency between the main façade and the layout of the rooms, which has remained a characteristic of the building to this day and is frequently mentioned in the literature. It may indicate that absolute priority was attached to the external appearance and its effect on the square. The sources imply that the Lotharingian architect Jean Nicolas de Jadot – who had moved from Tuscany to Vienna along with Franz I Stephan – was entrusted with the overall responsibility for the project.

Born in Lunéville (Lorraine) in 1710, Jadot was awarded the title "architecte ordinaire" of Duke Leopold of Lorraine in 1732. Little is known about his training and his works. He may have been a pupil of the Parisian architect Germain Boffrand, who designed several buildings in Lorraine, and may have received further training in Paris. In 1733 the Accademia Clementina in Bologna conferred on him the title "Accademico d'onore". In 1737 he moved to Florence where in 1738/1739 he designed the triumphal arch for the ceremonial entry of Franz Stephan as the new Grand Duke of Tuscany and was responsible for the inspection of the ducal buildings (including Palazzo Pitti). In 1745 he followed Franz Stephan, the husband of Maria Theresa, who had been crowned Emperor, to Vienna. Presumably, his main task was to draw up new plans for the Hofburg imperial residence. The plans of the architect, who had meanwhile risen to the rank of an Imperial "Bauinspector und Controlor", have never been realised. Still, Vienna boasts the three works definitively owed to Jadot: the Menagerie of Schönbrunn (including the vivarium and the central pavilion) of 1752, the Capuchin Crypt (1753) and the plans for the new university of the same year. A few weeks after the laying of the foundation stone for the latter on 10 August 1753, Jadot, however, left Vienna for Belgium. The architect, who had been raised to nobility (Baron de Ville-Issey), died in Lorraine in 1761.

After his departure from Vienna, the Imperial Royal Deputy Court architect Johann Adam Münzer as well as Johann Enzenhofer and Daniel Christoph Dietrich were entrusted with the execution of his model, plans and elevations. By 1755 the shell of the building, the roof and the observatory topping it as well as the fountains in the façade created by Franz Joseph Lenzbauer had been completed.

In the same year Gregorio Guglielmi and Domenico Francia finished their frescoes in the Great Hall, the central project of the building. The ceremonious inauguration of the university building took place on 5 April 1756. The interior decoration of the university was completed by the frescoes by Franz Anton Maulbertsch, the most important painter of late Austrian Baroque, in the Council Room (today "Museumszimmer") (1759) and in the lecture hall of the faculty of theology (today "Johannessaal", the Hall of John the Baptist) (1766/1767).

It took less than three years to complete the building. Construction work gave rise to criticism of – actual or alleged – shortcomings of Jadot's plans. The main critic was master builder Matthias Gerl, who as early as September 1754 published an expertise criticising the chimneys and parts of the interior decoration: the inadequate layout of the rooms and corridors, too thin partition walls, inadequate lighting of the halls and flat ceilings instead of vaulted ones. The main problem seems to have been that "[...] architect Jadot had worked along the principles of French palace architecture, where wood is the main building material for the residential areas, but which were in conflict with construction practices in Vienna, which relied on much more solid masonry and brick structures and vaults, and were subject to stringent building regulations. [...]" (Renate Wagner-Rieger).

This criticism did not remain unchallenged. One reaction – probably also driven by wounded pride – came from the Imperial

Court Architect Nikolaus Pacassi, who, in his expertise, took a firm position against Gerl's critical opinion. Master builder Gerl, it was basically claimed, was no graduate architect,

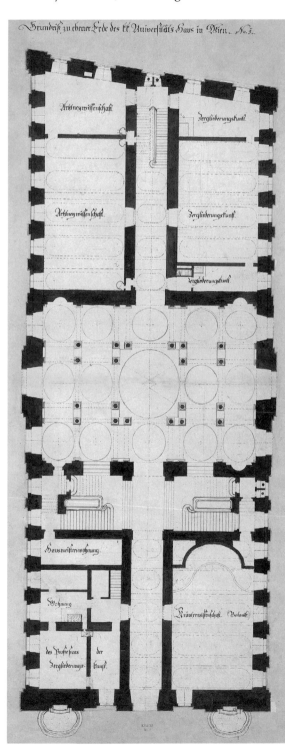

since "[...] he had not attended the academies, had not taken any examinations there, let alone received any official approbation [...]", and was thus unable to professionally assess the quality of Jadot's plans. The actual adaptations required would cost a mere 13 259 guilders rather than the 70 000 guilders estimated by Gerl. Pacassi's arguments were considered more credible, and the Empress thus entrusted him with the necessary work on 12 December 1757. These repairs were, however, not sufficient to overcome all the problems; even years later, in 1756, Pacassi was asked to furnish another opinion "[...] because of a number of indispensable repairs and adaptations required in the big university building" [...]". It is reported that Matthias Gerl was asked to submit a cost estimate also in this case, which turned out to be less expensive than the one submitted by Pacassi.

Plans and interior layout

From today's point of view the ground plan can be said to have achieved a reasonable equilibrium between function and space, offsetting the shortcomings of the narrow oblong building site. The layout of halls and rooms was determined by the space requirements for the academic activities and the wish to glorify the monarchs as sponsors of the sciences. None of the original plans drawn by Jadot himself have so far been discovered that would furnish detailed information on the spatial organisation and the original layout of the individual walls. The architecture collection of the Albertina

16

and the graphic collection of the Academy of Fine Arts in Vienna, however, possess a few sets of plans, all dating from the second half of the 18th century, from which reliable information can be gleaned.

These plans probably formed the basis for planned and actually realised adaptations, both around 1759, when the premises on the second floor were handed over to the Academy of Arts, and around 1786, when the

ACADEMY BUILDING AULA (FIG. 10)

Academy moved out again and the rooms were assigned to new scientific and administrative functions.

The Albertina Collection of Graphic Art possesses two sets of ground plans (basement, ground floor, main floor and second floor) and an elevation of the observatory, while the Academy of Fine Arts has among its holdings four interrelated drawings of one of its graduates, Architect Johann Georg Mack, dated November and December 1783 and January 1784: a plan of the ground floor, a façade elevation, a side elevation and a longitudinal section.

In contrast to what would normally have been expected, the layout of the interior is not derived from the organisation of the main façade but subordinated to the oblong shape of the building site (**Fig. 9**). The centre is a transverse space extending over the entire width of the plot (from Bäckerstrasse to Sonnenfelsgasse), which accommodates a colonnaded aula several aisles wide (**Fig. 10**) on the ground floor, and the Great Hall on the main floor above it (**Fig. 11**). The central aula is traversed by a longitudinal corridor with hardly any natural light, which stretches from the principal entrance on Dr. Ignaz Seipel Square to the rear entrance. As far as attempts at reconstructing the original plan suggest, the four roughly symmetrically arranged groups of rooms right and left of this longitudinal axis were assigned to the medical faculty. Following the ground plan as described by Johann Georg Mack, the two sets of rooms on the eastern side of the square (today the

ACADEMY BUILDING, GREAT HALL (FIG. 11)

19

BOTTOM LEFT:
PLAN OF THE
GROUND FLOOR OF
THE ACADEMY
BUILDING; VIENNA,
ALBERTINA, AZ.
ALLG. 8029 (FIG.12)

BOTTOM CENTER:
GROUND PLAN OF
THE MAIN STOREY
OF THE ACADEMY
BUILDING; VIENNA,
ALBERTINA, AZ.
ALLG. 8023 (FIG. 14)

porter's lodge and the mail room), i.e. to the left of the longitudinal corridor, were designated as "living quarters of the professor of anatomy" and, partitioned off from it, "porter's living quarters", while on the right-hand side was a five-bay, saucer-vaulted lecture hall assigned to the teaching of "herbal science (botany)" (today the "Club Room"). The rear of the building, the area behind the aula to the left of the corridor (today the library hall), was dedicated to pharmacology, the right-hand section (today the library administration) to anatomy. The latter department had at its disposal a four-bay hall accommodating the "anatomical theatre", which was even equipped with a lift to convey the bodies to be dissected from the basement into the lecture hall. One of the ground plans kept at the Albertina (**Fig. 12**) shows rows of seats forming an amphitheatre around a central dissecting table separated from the auditorium by a balustrade. When the Academy of Fine Arts moved out in 1786, the anatomical theatre was moved up to the second floor, not least on account of the poor lighting available on the ground floor. The ground-floor hall was subdivided into six rooms dedicated to anatomical studies.

The ground plan of the main floor, the piano nobile, is by and large similar to that of the ground floor. On the side of the square, in the south-eastern corner, there was the lecture hall for the faculty of theology, which is today called "Hall of John the Baptist" on account of its pictorial decoration (Baptism of Christ) (**Fig. 13**). Drawing No. 8023 (**Fig. 14**) in the Albertina collection already assigns this large hall (127m²) to "deology". Unlike today, it was directly accessible from the foyer of the Great Hall. If we follow another drawing in the Albertina (No. 8030) (**Fig. 15**), the theology hall was (unlike the situation on

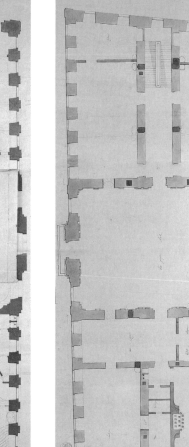
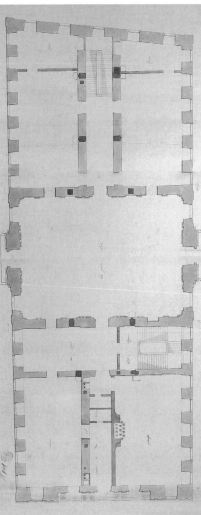

GROUND PLAN
OF THE MAIN
STOREY OF THE
ACADEMY
BUILDING;
VIENNA,
ALBERTINA,
AZ. ALLG. 8030
(FIG. 15)

the ground floor) not adjacent to a central corridor but to the large hall assigned to "philosofia". Plan No. 8023 (**see Fig. 14**), on the other hand, does show the wall necessary for forming the central corridor, which is, however, drawn in a different colour, a clear indication that this partition was added later. As a matter of fact, the building itself contains some clues that would support this view. Unlike the elegant saucer domes topping the other corridors (**Fig. 16**), the central corridor here shows only a modest barrel vault. Similarly, the vaulting of the Philosophy Hall (**Fig. 17**) is at variance with the vault types otherwise used by de Jadot: The light shallow barrel, which clashes with the deep conchae of the window bays, is a clear departure from the heavy vaulting used in the other halls of the building.

The Philosophy Hall (today the meeting hall of the two sections of the Academy), whose size was reduced by the later partitioning to 127 m², the same size as the Theology Hall, was formerly used as lecture hall for physics and mechanics and also accommodated a collection of physical instruments, artefacts and mechanical models.

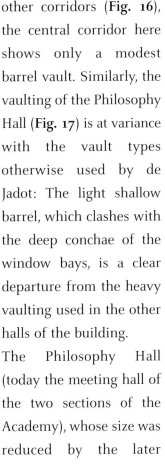

The rooms in the rear part of the building, designated as the "retirade" in our plan, were, according to Colland, used as lecture halls for law and the political sciences from 1796 onwards. After repeated modifications, they now accommodate the administration of the Academy and the rooms of its President.

As a transverse barrier the Great Hall, which extends over two storeys in height, separates the eastern and western parts of the building.

ACADEMY
BUILDING,
CENTRAL
CORRIDOR,
GROUND FLOOR
(FIG. 16)

With its size of more than 400 m² it divides the building into three largely separate sections (**see Fig. 11**). For practical purposes, this layout was, admittedly, not ideal: Direct communication between the parts of the building in which the lecture halls were located was only possible by passing through the Great Hall which, by its very nature, proved an obstacle to the conduct of day-to-day business. This problem is rendered even worse on the second floor, where the two parts dedicated to lecture halls are completely separated from one another on account of the height of the Great Hall. Incidentally, the second floor only became available to the faculties when the Academy of Fine Arts moved out in 1786. The area now reserved for administrative purposes was then used for the new anatomical theatre and for lecture halls for the departments of pathology, "materia medica" and obstetrics.

Access to the individual storeys is by three sets of stairs. The two principal stairs are embedded between the front part with the lecture halls on the side of the square and the central area with the aula and, above it, the Great Hall. Johann Georg Mack's longitudinal section (**Fig. 18**) clearly shows that this staircase section is to be seen as a structural unit in its own right: it is intercalated between the other parts of the building and, at its top, bears the observatory, which gives it a tower-like quality. The third staircase is in the rear part of the western central corridor (For the staircases, see also pp. 32, 33).

The Observatory

Ignaz de Luca's "Neuester wienerischer Wegweiser für Fremde und Inländer vom Jahr 1797 oder kurze Beschreibung aller Merkwürdigkeiten Wiens" (Short Guide to Vienna for Foreigners and Natives for the Year 1797 or Brief Description of all Sights of Vienna") recommends a visit to the university observatory: "[...] Ultimately, foreigners are especially advised to visit the observatory of

the university. It is perfectly equipped with all instruments required for astronomical observations. M. l'Abbé Driesneker, a disciple of the late M. l'Abbé Hell, Imperial Royal Court Astronomer, will most graciously receive foreigners and other scholars desirous of seeing or using the instruments and the observatory [...]".

The observatory, clearly visible on Johann Georg Mack's longitudinal section and elevation (**see Fig. 18 and Fig. 19**), was placed

ACADEMY BUILDING, MEETING ROOM (FORMER LECTURE HALL, FACULTY OF PHILOSOPHY) (FIG. 17)

23

J. G. MACK, FAÇADE
ELEVATION OF
THE ACADEMY
BUILDING, 1783/84;
VIENNA, AKADEMIE
DER BILDENDEN
KÜNSTE,
KUPFERSTICH-
KABINETT,
INV.-NO. 16718
(FIG. 19)

on top of the staircase section behind the hip roof on the side of the square, towering over it so as to impress its mark on the overall aspect of the building. A comparison with other pictures of the building from the late 18th and first half of the 19th century raises doubts as to the validity of the previous assumption that Bellotto's painting represented the original building as planned by de Jadot (**see Fig. 7**). In Mack's drawing, the platform with the large pavilion has at each corner a tower-like gazebo – which is also confirmed by Joseph Daniel Huber's bird's-eye view of Vienna (drawn 1769–1774) (**Fig. 20**). In 1879 the university observatory was moved to Türkenschanze

in the western part of Vienna. It is not known at what time the structures on top of the university building were dismantled. The only part of the superstructure that has survived is the platform.

Description of the building

One of the designer's principal objectives (**Fig. 21**) was for the façade to rival with, if not outstrip, the façade of the neighbouring church as the main visual attraction (**see Fig. 7**). While it was impossible to compete with the church façade in terms of height, its unassuming Early Baroque aspect invited competition, which persuaded the architect, Jean Nicolas de Jadot, to design an opulent yet noble façade.

At a first glance the building does not appear to be aimed to fit into, let alone submit to, the older buildings. The immediate surroundings were (and still are today) characterised by a quiet, even monotonous façade design such as was typical of urban construction in the 17th and early 18th centuries: flat façade subtly divided by stringcourses and reglets, partly with flat oriels and framed plaster fields. Outstanding plastic elements are confined to early 18th century window aediculae. Jadot's repertory of motifs is in utter contrast to these features: The three-storeyed building fronts along Bäckerstrasse and Sonnenfelsgasse (and, somewhat less pronounced, the rear facing Windhaaggasse) are characterised by the regular sequence of the ground-floor windows cut out from the fluted background and in particular the window aediculae with alternating round-arch and

triangular pediments along the piano nobile. The uniformity of the two lateral façades is only broken by a flat central three-bay projection with a central aedicula and balcony (**Fig. 22**).

Quite unlike the sparse direct application of decorative elements on the façade along the sides of the building, the façade facing the square is richly ornamented with columns and pilasters. However, some of these elements form part of a most elaborate system of organisation: On the side of the square, the wall of the five-bay façade is increasingly recessed from storey to storey. At the ground level, the ribbon structure forms the foremost, though very thin, layer which exposes, on the window and fountain arcades, the narrow but clearly discernible margin of the wall core, while the latter is carved out to form deep niches; the rear walls of the lateral fountain niches are deepened further by conchae (**Fig. 23**).

The Corinthian order on the piano nobile takes the form of an accessible colonnade which constitutes a spatial symbol of sovereignty in front of the deeply recessed central wall. On the third storey, finally, the façade with the three central bays is also recessed, with a balustraded balcony flanked by two lateral projections replacing the colonnade of the storey below.

The four fronts of the free-standing building show a clear hierarchical organisation reflecting their functions. The fairly simple decorative pattern along the short

ACADEMY BUILDING, PRINCIPAL FAÇADE (FIG. 21)

façade fronting the square, and its location corresponds externally to the central projections of the two lateral façades. It is this absence of a genuine connection between the splendour of the façade and the interior that demonstrates the architect's intention to set off the façade from the university building behind it in order to enter upon a direct dialogue with the predetermined features of the square. The first thing one tends to note is that the height of the university building is similar to that of the Jesuit College opposite (**Fig. 24**). The storeys by and large correspond to each other in height (one important difference being that the height of the piano nobile of the

Windhaaggasse lane is enriched on the two longitudinal fronts and culminates – rather surprisingly for a structure built in the latter part of the 18th century – in a magnificent façade reminiscent of a Baroque mis-en-scene. What all four fronts have in common is a basic repertoire of decorative elements (dominant stringcourses, aediculae with triangular pediments and pedimented windows with cartouches) that emphasises homogeneity and ensures that the architect's message is easily read.

As the ground plan of the piano nobile (see **Fig. 15**) shows clearly, the noble, triumphal colonnade architecture of the principal façade has but little to do with the interior structure of the building. The splendid Great Hall, situated in the central part of the building, is completely independent of the

DR. IGNAZ SEIPEL-
PLATZ WITH
THE ACADEMY
BUILDING, THE
JESUIT CHURCH
AND THE JESUIT
COLLEGE
(FIG. 24)

Aula corresponds to the combined second and third storeys of the College). Another important aspect is that the axial division of the university front is inspired by that of the church façade (**see Fig. 5**): both consist of two flat single-bay lateral projections and a three-bay central portion. Both the respect for the proportions of the earlier building forming the counterpart and the transposition of the basic five-part rhythm, give rise to the minimum of harmony required to form a solid basis for a design after all characterised by considerable differences in approach. Similarly, the alternation of rounded and triangular window pediments used by Jadot may be interpreted as the architect's deliberate response to the decorative elements of the church façade. Jadot can use the sculptural and spatial design of the façade to produce an aesthetic effect which challenges, as it were, the unachievable height of the church front with its monumental storeys,

the massive gable and ornate steeple roofs, creating a more than adequate counterpoise to the flat and almost two-dimensional organisation of the Early Baroque church façade. The spatial effect of the dominant colonnade (historically taking its cue from the east façade of the Paris Louvre) is a first-rate expression of dignified authority. The viewer may even go farther than Renate Wagner-Rieger, who speaks of "Erscheinungsarchitektur" (architecture of appearance), and interpret the principal façade as triumphal theatre-like architecture, perhaps intended for the Emperor and Empress to present themselves to the public on the occasion of university celebrations on the square.

The imagery of the façade (**see Fig. 21**) is sparse. The peculiar grotesque faces on the bosses and the groups of statues adorning the fountains on the ground floor can hardly be interpreted as fitting into the university context. At the level of the principal floor

there are empty coat-of-arms cartouches and
eagles carrying trophies. As regards the third-
floor allegorical sculptures representing the
various faculties above the triangular
pediments, it is not entirely clear whether
they were not meant to stand for the two
originally envisaged faculties, medicine (left)
and jurisprudence (right) (**Fig. 25, Fig. 26**),
whose attributes were subsequently altered
in view of the addition of two more faculties.
At the centre above the attic, the dominion
of the monarch who commissioned the
structure is documented by the monumental
imperial coat of arms representing the
alliance between the houses of Habsburg and
Lorraine (**Fig. 27**), the small escutcheons
between the two faculty groups – with the
coat of arms of Neu-Österreich on the left
and probably that of Alt-Österreich on the
right [today empty] – and the coats of arms
above the side portals, that of the Kingdom
of Hungary (**Fig. 28**) in Bäckerstrasse and of

FRANCISCUS I. MARIA THERESIA AUGG:
SCIENTIIS ET ARTIB: RESTITUT: POSUERUNT. MDCCLIIII

the Kingdom of Bohemia in Sonnenfelsgasse
(**Fig. 29**). The territorial claim of the
university was succinctly characterised by
Ignaz de Luca in 1797: "[...] Vienna and the
Austrian universities in general certainly do
not intend to attract foreign students; their
attention is focused merely on educating
young men of local origin and leading them
to the source of scholarship so that the State
may assign them usefully to its offices and
provide its people with adequate culture and
refinement. And that is enough [...]".

The prestigious interior

The Stairs

The Principal Entrance gives on to a central corridor which has five bays topped by saucer domes and at its end leads to two flights of stairs right and left (**Fig. 30**). On either side a few steps lead up to raised platforms which lend additional significance to the stairs that rise from them. Surprisingly, the two stairs differ in design. Apparently the architect intended to distinguish them both functionally and typologically.

ACADEMY
BUILDING,
STAIRCASE
LANDING
(FIG. 30)

The right-hand flight of stairs, on the side of Sonnenfelsgasse, passes in three sections with two landings around six slender piers up to the first and second floors. It has heavy stone balustrades and is topped by a sequence of shallow saucer domes (**Fig. 31**). Strikingly, the staircase arcades are not aligned with the window openings. The fact that the arcades do not correspond to the windows in the façade facing Sonnenfelsgasse can hardly be assumed to have been intended by as high-calibre an architect as Jean Nicolas de Jadot. Much rather, the faulty alignment is likely to be due to the fact that the execution of the stairs did not follow the original plan. The other stairway – the one on the south side along Bäckerstrasse – is neatly fitted into the basic structure of the building and is comparatively sumptuous in aspect (**Fig. 32**). It also features three sections and has a well extending over the entire height of the first upper floor. Its alignment with the window openings ensures that the splendid white stairway is steeped in light, which enhances the impression of openness and serenity. Both stairs lead up to a three-bay foyer (**Fig. 33**) in front of the Great Hall, from which it is separated by three arches.

The typological distinction between "stairway" and "staircase" corresponds to a hierarchical one, which in turn reflects a functional difference. The more elaborate

There is yet a third, inconspicuous staircase serving, for the most part, practical purposes. It branches off the western part of the central corridor, has two steep sections separated by corbelled landings and gives access to the lecture halls at the three levels of the rear part of the building.

ACADEMY BUILDING, NORTHERN STAIRCASE (FIG. 31)

ACADEMY BUILDING, SOUTHERN STAIRCASE, LEFT SIDE (FIG. 32)

"stairway" was intended for solemn events in the Great Hall, while the more modest staircase up to the second floor served humbler purposes such as everyday activities of the university and gave access to the lecture halls at all three levels in the part of the building facing the square.

ACADEMY BUILDING, FOYER ON
MAIN STOREY (FIG. 33)

The ground-floor Aula

The space between the stairs that branch
off from the central corridor and the rear
part of the building gives access to a
splendid colonnaded hall consisting of five
aisles of three bays each (**see Fig. 10**). Set
off against the longitudinal axis, it forms a
transverse element reflected on the exterior
in the central projections with their three
large entrances that divide the street fronts
of the building. The entrances originally

PERFORMANCE OF JOSEPH HAYDN'S "THE CREATION", WATERCOLOUR BY B. WIGAND (1808) (FIG. 34)

PORTRAIT OF
GREGORIO
GUGLIELMI,
MEZZOTINT BY J.
E. HAID AFTER
ARTIST'S OWN
DRAWING
(FIG. 35)

served to admit, and provide exits for, carriages, as the small proportions of the building site prevented the construction of a courtyard. Without any doubt, the generous dimensions of the hall are at least in part due to the need for this dual function as a prestigious aula and carriage house.

Coupled Doric columns support fifteen flat domes the longitudinal orientation of which is enhanced by oval plaster frames. The central bay at the intersection of the building's main axis and the middle one of the three transverse axes is widened and enclosed at the corners by four groups of three columns placed at right angles. This wide central bay forms the geometric middle not only of the colonnaded hall but of the entire building. Exactly above it, in the Great Hall on the principal floor, is the centre of the ceiling fresco.

The Great Hall

As long as the building accommodated the university, the Great Hall was used for the election of the University Chancellor as well as for disputations and other solemn functions (**see Fig. 11**). On 27 March 1808 it saw the first performance of Joseph Haydn's "The Creation" conducted by Court Conductor Salieri, as depicted in a water colour by Balthasar Wigand (**Fig. 34**). The aged composer was

GREGOIRE GUGLIELMI
Peintre en Histoires tres Celebre,
né à Rome Le 13. Decembre 1714.

taken to the university in a princely carriage and carried up to the Great Hall in a lavishly decorated sedan chair. Today the Hall serves as venue for important events of the Austrian Academy of Sciences.

The ceiling fresco was executed by Gregorio Guglielmi (1714–1773) (**Fig. 35**), who was commissioned on the recommendation of Pietro Metastasio (1698–1782) (**Fig. 36**), who had met Guglielmi in Dresden in 1753 and was the author of the pictorial programme.

Gregorio Guglielmi

Gregorio Guglielmi had studied with Sebastiano Conca and became a member of the "Accademia di San Luca" in 1748. According to the records he was in Dresden in 1753 and in Turin in 1759, and took part in the decoration of the Small and Large Galleries of Schönbrunn Palace (1761/1762). His renown took him to many places throughout Europe, as is evidenced, amongst other things, by the ceiling paintings in the Grand Hall of the Schäzler Palace at Augsburg. By 1772 he was working in St. Petersburg, and in the same year he became a member of the "Accademia de Disegno" in Florence. Like Luca Giordano, Gregorio Guglielmi was the typical migrant artist who executed decorative work of different kinds in all parts of Europe.

The pictorial programme

In early 1755 Cardinal Prince-Archbishop Johann Josef Graf von Trautson, the Protector of the University, addressed a letter to the Imperial Court Poet Pietro Metastasio, asking him to draft the literary programme for a large ceiling fresco to decorate the hall of the new University Building (**Fig. 37**). While this letter has been lost, Metastasio's reply of February or March 1955 has survived. In it, the poet outlines the basics of the programme. One of Metastasio's chief demands was that the painting be iconographically unequivocal, so that even the "man in the street" ("qualunque più rozzo spettatore") would understand what the fresco meant. At the very beginning of his letter, Pietro Metastasio outlines the two central subjects of the programme. As regards the university schools or faculties, his wish is that their representation should be noble and should show, as clearly as possible, which fields of study were to be pursued by the university: "[...] Uno. Il dimostrare con la nobiltà e con la chiarezza possibile quali siano le scienze che si coltivano nell'università suddetta. [...]".

The long sides of the ceiling show the Faculties of Theology and Jurisprudence, while the more modest narrow sides are dedicated to the other two faculties. The fresco devoted to the Faculty of Theology

occupies the area facing the main entrance. Metastasio's letter describes in detail how the individual faculties are to be represented. Accordingly, the viewer is given first-hand information by a brief designation (on a painted marble tablet) of the school in question: "Theology" ("DIVINARVM RERVM NOTITIA" [Knowledge of Things Divine]), "Jurisprudence" ("IVSTI ATQUE INIVSTI SCIENTIA" [Science of the Just and the Unjust]), "Philosophy" ("CAVSARVM INVESTIGATIO" [Investigation of Causes]) and "Medicine" ("ARS TVENDAE ET REPARANDAE VALETVDINIS" [Art of the Protection and Recovery of Health]). The tablets are flanked by angels and genii painted in grisaille.

Thematically, the ceiling design is rounded off by vases and architectural elements peopled by a variety of figures in historical and contemporary costumes. The corners contain painted allegories of the four continents and their principal rivers (Danube, Ganges, Nile and Rio de la Plata). In this way the "universality" of human knowledge is visualised in line with the traditional system of groups of four. In its present form, the ceiling fresco in the Great Hall of the Austrian Academy of Sciences is not the original but a reconstruction: A fire on 7 and 8 February 1961 completely

programme – the original plan envisaged only one figure, that of "Fama" (with a trombone), to proclaim the glory of Maria Theresa.

The Ceiling Centre (Fig. 39)

The zenith of the ceiling bears an oval medallion with profile portraits of the Imperial couple, Franz I Stephan and Maria Theresa, surrounded by three figures: that of Chronos, a huge hoary old man with spread wings, holding in his hands an upright oval tablet bearing the portraits. That the medallion is placed in the hands of the God of Time serves as an admonition to keep the memory of the celebrated monarchs for all times. Opposite Chronos, a cherub kneeling on a dark cloud and surrounded by a drape holds in his left hand an olive branch, while his right supports the portrait medallion. In front of him hovers an eagle, its talons grasping the fragments of a scythe, the attribute of Chronos. In allegory, the eagle signifies Temporality overwhelmed by Eternity – time "superseded" by the eternal quality of lasting fame. Above, a little angel holds a laurel wreath in his left hand. The original pictorial programme envisaged five figures around the medallion with the portraits of Maria Theresa and Franz I: Chronos, the eagle and the three cherubs carrying the olive branch, the laurel and a serpent with its tail in its mouth (the "Ouroboros" as a symbol of eternity). Possibly, the cherub with the serpent was left out in the final version because the

destroyed the ceiling fresco of Gregorio Guglielmi and the quadraturist Domenico Francia (1702–1758). Otto Demus, President of the Federal Office for the Protection of Monuments, strongly advocated restoring the fresco to its original state. The arduous work was executed by the academic painter Paul Reckendorfer and his staff within less than two years.

A pen drawing with watercolour wash dating from 1754/1755 (**Fig. 38**) kept at the Wien Museum is likely to be one of the earliest general sketches for Guglielmi's ceiling fresco (1754/1755). Unlike the version ultimately executed, this drawing relegated "Theology" and "Jurisprudence" to the narrow sides of the hall. Considerable differences between the drawing and the executed fresco are also found in the centre, where – in contrast to Metastasio's

GREAT HALL,
CEILING FRESCO,
CENTRE
(THE IMPERIAL
COUPLE)
(FIG. 39)

personification of Eternity was already symbolised by the broken scythe of Chronos.

"Theology" (Fig. 40)

The background is formed by a domed circular structure with Corinthian pilasters. A bearded old man in a bright robe (possibly John the Evangelist) sits on a pedestal in front of it, holding in his left a tablet with the inscription "In principio erat verbVm" from the Prologue of the Gospel according to St. John (John 1, 1). The central figure and two youthful figures flanking it, holding a cross (right) and censer (left), form the top of a pyramid on the sides of which there are groups of men apparently in a state of agitation. The two dominant figures – preachers – probably symbolise the preaching of Gospel by the Apostles. The preacher on the right is addressing a group of

avid listeners, the one on the left is facing an audience that appears, at least at first sight, to be unwilling to listen. The base is formed by a carpet spread over the stairs strewn with precious liturgical objects. The lower corners show a representative of "Tradition" (the author of the Acts of the Apostles?) with an open book and a pen (but without specific attributes) and what might perhaps be a "historian", while playing cherubs form the front edge of the foreground. The sides are peopled by groups of men along the balustrades engaged in disputation. The group of scholars to their right evidently includes representatives of "Speculation". And the third sub-discipline of Religion envisaged in the programme, "[...] which is imprinted in our souls by Nature [...]", appears to have been depicted as representatives of Greek paganism, Islam and one representative of the heathen peoples.

"Jurisprudence" (Fig. 41)

The background is a decorative stage architecture with half-pillars and pilasters forming a semicircle. As in the case of the "Theology" allegory, richly draped figures form a pyramidal structure at the top of which a young man holds a stone tablet on which the eighth "tabula" of the Roman Law of the Twelve Tables is inscribed ("SI QVADRVPES / PAVPERIEM SARCITO / QVI FRVGES / EXCANTASIT / ENDO"). To the left, another group studies and discusses the laws of the first "tabula", whose contents are summarised in the form of individual

keywords ("SI IN IVS VOCAT / QVEAT / NI IT ANTESTA[mino] / IGITVR ENCI / SI CALVITVR / PEDEMVE [...]"). On the steps below the central figure, four old men are absorbed in the study of the Twelve Tables and Emperor Justinian I's "Corpus iuris civilis" or explain its contents to those around them. An open volume of the Justinian Corpus lies on the steps, showing the definition of "Iustitia" from the "Institutiones" (I,1) of the "Corpus iuris civilis" ("IVSTITIA EST / CONSTA[N]S / ET PERPE[TUA] / VO[LUNTAS] IVS SVVM / [CVIQUE TRIBUENDI]"). In accordance with Metastasio's programme, Roman Law is represented as embodied in the Twelve Tables, and a distinction is made between the "natural law" of the peoples and "civil law". The poet's proposal for the representation of "natural law" was, however, not taken up

by the artist – possibly because its realisation would have required a host of symbols and allegorical allusions. The group on the right side has for its focus two figures in the company of a man – ostensibly a dignitary, as can be seen from his chain and medal – holding an open book. The left-hand group shows an assembly of scholars engaged in various activities, possibly representatives of "natural law", which had been admitted as an academic subject as late as 1753 in connection with the extensive reforms undertaken by Maria Theresa. A man holding scrolls (with seal cases attached) may well be a representative of modern law ("feudal law" and "the law governing the Habsburg lands").

GREAT HALL, CEILING FRESCO, JURISPRUDENCE (FIG. 41)

"Philosophy" (Fig. 42)

Various set pieces – a temple in ruins, a pyramid and a massive rock – form the background of the scene. The pyramid (obelisk), in this context the symbol of the central contents and objectives of philosophy – steadfastness and wisdom –, calls to mind Piranesi's famous engravings of the Pyramid of Cestius in Rome. At the centre of the scene there is a large globe. Stooping over it, an old man in classical contrapposto extends his right arm in a donnish gesture. Obviously the allusion is to "Geography". In the left foreground, two young men study an apparatus – a clockwork with a horizontal axis mounted on a plate. Behind them are three old men, earnest and unmoving in their white togas, in all probability Greek philosophers. The right-hand side is dominated by the figure of a physicist manipulating the levers of some

apparatus; behind him is another old man wearing a headband identifying him as an antique scholar, while the rest of the background is made up of figures bearing no insignia or attributes. The rock on the right-hand side of the centre ground is assigned to "Astronomy": three astronomers are handling a huge refractor (a telescope with several convex lenses), with one of them looking through it to observe the sky.

"Medicine" (Fig. 43)

The centre of the scene is a dissecting table on which a greenish corpse is shown with amputated arms and an opened trunk. Below the table there is a metal bowl from which a sawn-off leg protrudes; by its side lies a bone saw. In line with Metastasio's programme, this central part is flanked by the ancillary disciplines "Botany" (right) and "Chemistry" (as well as "Mineralogy" [left]). While, on the left, a number of miners armed with pickaxes are labouring to wrest from the earth substances beneficial to humanity, people on the right are busying themselves collecting bundles of herbs, which stand for the importance of the vegetable kingdom for the medical sciences. Indeed, it was on account of Gerard van Swieten's (1700–1772) (**Fig. 44**) reform of medical studies of 1749 that "Botany" and "Chemistry" had been introduced as new disciplines.

The overall design of the ceiling fresco

Before the backdrop of the comprehensive reforms of all disciplines, Metastasio's programme and its execution by Guglielmi in the Great Hall of the university building reflect iconographically a decisive step in the development of university studies: from the Early Modern Age, when the faculties were defined in biblical and theological terms, to the "modern" interpretation of scientific disciplines inspired by the Age of Enlightenment and reflected in contemporary university reforms. The rapid development of the various branches of scholarship and science in the 18th century confronted the iconography of scholarship with new tasks that went far beyond its traditional scope. No longer were the customary concepts capable of adequately representing the current state of the sciences and their diversification. The

GERARDVS L. B. VAN SWIETEN
Augg. Imperatoris et Imperatricis a consiliis, Archiater cam. Bibliothecæ
Augustæ Præfectus, incl. Fac. Med. Vienn. Præses perpetuus, Acad. reg.
Scient. et chir. Paris. Instit. Bonon. et Lit. ercogent Membrum.
nat. Lugd. Bat. VI non. Maji MDCC.

requirements of visualising the significance of the divers fields of knowledge for everyday life greatly surpasses the possibilities of a strictly codified iconology such as it was handed down in the relevant manuals of the 17th and 18th centuries.

In Guglielmi's fresco the traditional personifications of "Faith", "Religion", "Justice" and "Medicine" are replaced by a highly realistic, practice-oriented concept which emphasises the tenet that science is rooted in life itself. This is most clearly visible in the depiction of the dissection of a body. Metastasio's scholarly concetto posed almost insurmountable difficulties for Guglielmi in his efforts to translate these concepts into the language of art. How was he to find convincing imagery for such concepts as "Natural Religion" and "Revealed Religion", "Tradition" and "Speculation"? The artistic representation of "Philosophy", too, all but overtaxed the artist: He was expected to find a pictorial expression not only for "Metaphysics" and "Ethics" but also for the exploration of Earth and of celestial bodies.

It was probably Archbishop Trautson's way of thinking that prompted the development of this concept: As Protector of the University, he was closely involved in the reforms undertaken in the curricula of theology, philosophy and jurisprudence. What is more, in his famous pastoral letter

GREAT HALL,
GROUP OF
STATUES BY J. G.
MÜLLER, ALIAS
MOLLINAROLO,
"LIBERALITY"
(FIG. 45)

of 1752 he had already opposed, amongst other practices, the overly frequent use of allegories – popular as they were especially in the age of Baroque. The integration of the positive and historical disciplines of theology as well as the inclusion of natural law in the academic curriculum – so convincingly realised in the iconography of the fresco – can be traced to his initiative. Similarly, the natural science curricula were also thoroughly reformed; here, the decisive impulses were due to van Swieten, the president of the medical faculty.

The sculptural programme

The intentions of the pictorial programme are underscored both by the four major groups of statues in the wall niches of the Great Hall (created by Jakob Gabriel Müller, also known as Mollinarolo (1721–1780) [as pointed out by Luigi A. Ronzoni]) and the eight pairs of cherubs on the entablatures of the four central projections above the coupled pilasters.

The four large – extremely slender – rhythmically agitated groups in the niches are executed as an interesting mix of free-standing statues and high reliefs, since they are connected with the curved rear wall up to two thirds of their total height. Thematically, they refer to the principal subject of the hall decoration, the allegorical representation of the Habsburg rule: the group left of the entrance represents "Wisdom" and "Vigilance" (symbolised by a mirror and oil lamp), while the right-hand group shows "Liberality" (two women handing out coins from bowls) (**Fig. 45**). In addition to these groups, which represent properties traditionally attributed to rulers, the opposite sides feature "Faith", "Constancy" and "Fortitude" as personifications of spiritual and temporal power (with a two-bar cross and a marshal's baton as their attributes (**Fig. 46**) as well as "Peaceable and Martial Power" (with a book as well as a crown and sword as their respective attributes). Along with thematically related festoons which had formerly been affixed to the walls and have recently been mounted again in

HALL OF JOHN THE
BAPTIST, CEILING
FRESCO, F. A.
MAULBERTSCH,
CA. 1766/67
(FIG. 47)

their original places, they formulate a unitary concept which is also reflected, on the entablature, by at least some of the pairs of cherubs, which refer back to the various faculties shown in the pictorial programme. It is here that painting and sculpture merge to form a conceptual unity which adds to the effect of the overall programme – the apotheosis, in allegorical form, of the virtues of the Habsburg monarchs and the sponsorship of the sciences by the Imperial couple, Franz I Stephan and Maria Theresa.

The Hall of John the Baptist

Next to the one in the Great Hall, the most important pictorial ensemble decorating the interior of the university building is found in the Hall of John the Baptist, originally a lecture hall of the Faculty of Theology. No documents regarding the execution of the fresco (**see Fig. 13, Fig. 47**) have survived. The earliest mention is found in a notice in the "Allergnädigst privilegierter Anzeiger" of 18 September 1771. Probably the fresco was painted in the late sixties. The artist was Franz Anton Maulbertsch, born at Langenargen on Lake Constance in 1724 (**Fig. 48**), the most important painter of the second half of the 18th century in Austria and as likely as not the outstanding Central European fresco painter of his time. His rich Œuvre, like that of none of his contemporaries, encompasses all the various stylistic currents in Baroque painting. Maulbertsch is believed to have been a pupil of Peter van Roy (Royen) and, from 1741, Jakob van Schuppen. His chief works in Vienna were the frescoes in the Piarist Church (1752/1753) and the ceiling fresco "Maria Theresa founding the Order of St. Stephen" in the Council Hall of the Hungarian Embassy in Vienna (1766–1769), which recommended him for the most challenging task of decorating the Hall of John the Baptist. In fact, his name was by that time well known to those in charge of the project, since he had, in 1759, painted the fresco (today unfortunately in very poor condition) in what is now the

"Museumszimmer", then the Council Room of the Academy of Fine Arts, which was temporarily accommodated in the building.

The decoration of the Hall of John the Baptist relies solely on the art of painting. Even though renovated several times, the mural decoration has remained very faithful to the original plan. The hollow moulding above the cornice is accentuated by cartouches at the centre of the sides and in the corners. The decorative border on the narrow side, through which one now enters the hall, originally framed the lecturer's rostrum, while the entrance was through a – now walled-up – door from the vestibule. The painted dome at the centre of the decorative border was exactly above the rostrum. The wall originally containing the entrance to the hall shows a trompe-l'œil architectural design framing an oval field dedicated to the painted personification of the Church ("Ecclesia" with the Sealed Book) and the New Covenant symbolised by the Chalice with the Host.

Guglielmi's fresco in the Great Hall was still governed by the principles of traditional Baroque fresco painting: the painted, illusionistic architecture widening the actual space is intended for an onlooker who stands at the centre of the room, looking upwards. While ceiling frescoes were still to be painted towards the end of the 18th century, these later paintings dispensed with spatial illusion and gave the impression of framed pictures sharply distinguished from the architectural features of the room. Stylistically, the

fresco in the Hall of John the Baptist holds an intermediate position between Baroque illusion and the new approach to pictorial ceiling decoration.

Like a mural, but perhaps less consistently, this fresco consists of a bottom zone and the sky above. The scene, which extends along the border and around the corners to the centre of the hall, is still reminiscent of the principle of the viewer standing at the centre below. This contradiction imbues the scene – a rocky landscape grown with bushes and

HALL OF JOHN THE BAPTIST, CEILING FRESCO BY F. A. MAUL-BERTSCH, CA. 1766/67, DETAIL (BAPTISM) (FIG. 49)

trees (**Fig. 47, 49, 50**) – with something of the irreality of a fairy world. While most scenes of baptism traditionally show only a few people attending the ceremony, the large area to be painted seems to have persuaded Maulbertsch to break with this tradition. Accordingly, his Baptism of Christ exploits the painter's full repertoire and shows a large number of decoratively arranged spectators, some of whom are shedding their clothes in preparation for being baptised.

The two principal figures, Christ and the Baptist, are given prominence: John stands on a cliff, Christ, praying, is placed above the river or rather a cataract which forms a kind of pedestal from which the figure of Christ rises, forming an impressive contrast with the falling waters. The Father, with extended arms and surrounded by angels, floats above the dove – the Holy Spirit – and the heavenly light emanating from it cascades down onto Christ and focuses the viewer's attention onto Him.

The lightness of the original colour scheme has been faithfully recaptured by a recent restoration. The rocks are so bright as not to compete for attention with the clouds. The woman with child and the oriental sitting behind her are exemplary of Maulbertsch's skill in handling colour. The yellow of the oriental's brocade mantle is brightened to such an extent that the colour is almost swallowed by the radiant light, and the same also holds for the figure of the woman. As regards the group on the other side, it takes a second look to discover that what at first

seemed but one figure is in reality two: an oriental swathed in an ornate wind-blown garment, and behind him another figure with a raspberry-red cap; in front of the two, a reclining young cavalier. By the use of colour, artificial postures and billowing garments Maulbertsch transforms his figures and groups into decorative elements. Independently of the actual shapes of the individual figures, he creates decorative configurations which blend far better into the overall composition than would correctly drawn figures. In its ethereal lightness and emphasis on decoration, the fresco recalls

HALL OF JOHN THE BAPTIST, CEILING FRESCO BY F. A. MAULBERTSCH, CA. 1766/67, DETAIL (FIG. 50)

Maulbertsch's early Œuvre from the fifties, while the perfect precision of his draughtsmanship already heralds the classicist style of his later works.

The Theological Faculty were customarily represented allegorically or by saints such as Thomas Aquinas or Catherine of Alexandria. That it was decided in the sixties of the 18th century to replace this imagery by the Baptism of Christ was probably due to the perceived need to make the pictorial programmes of frescoes more comprehensible, as evidenced in Metastasio's exemplary programme for the Great Hall. Surprisingly, Maulbertsch's fresco does not show John as he baptises Jesus: The Baptist extends his arms, overwhelmed by the revelation of Christ as the Son of God. The painter here adheres closely to the wording in the Gospel according to St. John, the only one that relates that John the Baptist actually saw the Holy Spirit descending on Jesus and, as the text stresses, "abiding upon him" (John 1, 32 et seq.). It is the resulting complete and permanent possession of the Spirit (John 1, 33) that is the foremost characteristic of the Messiah. While the act of baptising is not actually depicted, it is seen as a necessary prerequisite and context of the moment shown by the painter.

Historically, the iconography of the Baptism of Christ in the Hall of John the Baptist is closely connected with the objectives of teaching at the Theological Faculty of the University of Vienna after 1752 – the time when great efforts were made to undermine the monopoly of the Jesuits and to fight their traditional scholastic theology by a kind of short-term alliance between Augustinianism and Thomism. Maulbertsch's visualisation of baptism as the revelation of Holy Trinity becomes more transparent once we take into account the significant position of this sacrament in contemporary textbooks and academic disputations. Thus, the ceiling fresco cannot be properly understood unless one is familiar with the contemporary discussions of the central issues of baptismal and trinitarian theology. It reflects thematically the doctrines of the Augustinians and the Dominicans and their strong opposition to every and any form of Antitrinitarianism, that prevailed from 1752 or, at the latest, from 1759 when the Jesuits were ousted from the Vienna theological faculty. On account of the perceived need to demonstrate beyond any doubt his opposition to antitrinitarian heresies, the painter deliberately refrained from visualising, in the form of a narrative, a Biblical report or a parable; rather, he clearly highlighted, through the Baptism of Christ, the central message of Catholic revealed religion as it can be derived from the first chapter of the Gospel of John.

The Academy of Sciences – the development
of an Austrian research institution

The edifice originally built by Maria Theresa for the university has been home to the Austrian Academy of Sciences since 1857.

In comparison with other academies in Europe and, in particular, in other German-speaking countries, the history of the Austrian Academy of Sciences is rather short. It was founded as the Imperial Academy of Sciences in 1847. However, plans for such an Imperial Academy are actually documented from the beginning of the 18th century. Gottfried Wilhelm Leibniz (1646–1716), who had founded an academy in Berlin in 1700, strongly advocated a similar undertaking in Vienna, where he stayed from 1712 to 1714. Although he obtained the necessary Imperial approval, the realisation of his project failed. The famous philosopher strove to arouse the interest and active participation of influential people in his plans for a "society" for the sciences. The Emperor received him in audience in early 1713 and promised to appoint him Director of a future academy. Even after his departure from Vienna, Leibniz made great efforts to implement his ambitious plan and corresponded with various official and scholarly personalities, amongst them – up to his death – with Prince Eugene of Savoy. When Leibniz died, a group of Austrian scholars headed by the Imperial historiographer and dramatist Apostolo Zeno (1688–1750) sought, apparently with the support of Emperor Charles VI, to pursue the idea of establishing an academy. A similar proposal came from abroad: In 1749 Professor Johann Christoph Gottsched, of Leipzig, advocated the establishment of a "German society", and in the same year the Austrian Freiherr Joseph von Petrasch, who had caught the attention of the academic world in 1746 by founding the "Societas eruditorum incognitorum in terris Austriacis" at Olmütz (Olomouc), also submitted a petition for the foundation of an "Akademie der Wissenschaften, Künste und angenehmen Kenntnisse". Neither proposal survived the preliminary stage, since they did not fit into Maria Theresa's more practice-oriented plans. The same can be said about a project discussed in the 1870's among members of the Imperial Studienhofkommission to found an academy in the broader context of a general reorganisation of Austria's system of education, which also met with the Empress's displeasure.

Maria Theresa's successor, Emperor Joseph II, who ruled from 1780 to 1790, concentrated even more than his mother on practical and utilitarian reforms, so that the establishment of an Academy by authority of the state was hardly feasible. This situation persisted in the early years of the rule of Emperor Franz II (Franz I of Austria) (from 1792 to 1835), who faced the overwhelming problems of a state budget completely out of control and had to finance the war against Napoleon. In the Vormärz (Pre-March) era, efforts to establish an institution devoted to scientific research were renewed, and in 1810 the renowned historian Joseph Freiherr von Hormayr von Hortenburg (1781[?]–1848) took up the idea of an Academy that was to encompass the whole of the Empire. With a petition addressed to the Imperial Court and signed by twelve scholars led by the orientalist and historian, Joseph Freiherr von Hammer-Purgstall (1774–1856), efforts to found an Academy took more concrete shape in 1837. By that time institutions of a similar nature had long existed in other parts of the Empire: there was the Royal Bohemian Society for the Sciences in Prague, founded as early as 1776, the Hungarian Academy in Budapest (1825) and, from 1836 onwards, the South Slavic Academy of Sciences at Agram (Zagreb).

It was Hammer-Purgstall who proposed that a petition to be addressed to Emperor Ferdinand I should be formulated. It was ultimately submitted to Archduke Ludwig on 20 March 1837. Although many experts favoured the ambitious project, it was not implemented, but State Chancellor Metternich still kept it in mind. Ten years later, in 1847, the Academy was established at long last. This was due to Metternich's positive attitude and the great strides scientific knowledge – in particular in the natural

sciences and medicine – had made in Austria in the ten years from 1837 to 1847. The proliferation and wide dissemination of liberal writings had brought about a marked change in Austria's intellectual climate, and from 1846 onwards Metternich himself repeatedly pleaded for the creation of an Imperial Royal Academy of Sciences – most emphatically in a submission to the Emperor dated 13 January 1846, in which he stated, amongst other things: "[...] I submit a proposal for the establishment of an Imperial Royal Academy of Sciences to be erected at Your Majesty's capital of the realm. [...] Truths are and remain the same at all ages! Time merely has an influence on their recognition and the greater or lesser value attached to their realisation. What I am taking the liberty of proposing today I first suggested already many years ago, when conditions were different from what they are now. [...]". The date of the Imperial approval of these petitions submitted by the State Chancellor, 14 May 1847, is considered the "founding date" of the Academy. Initially, 40 ordinary members (17 of the mathematical and natural-sciences section and 23 of the historical-philological section, subsequently redesignated philosophic-historical section), among them representatives from Lombardy and Venetia as well as Bohemia and Hungary. In addition to the ordinary members there were also 72 corresponding members, 36 from the Monarchy and 36 from abroad, as well as 24 honorary members, 8 from the Monarchy and 16 foreign ones. On 27 June

Hammer.Purgstall was elected first President of the Academy. Its statutes were approved by Emperor Ferdinand on 23 November 1847.

The rededication of the University building to the Academy of Sciences

Initially the Academy had to make do with temporary accommodation in the rooms of the Polytechnic Institute, today the Vienna University of Technology. Ceremonial meetings were held in the Great Hall of Niederösterreichisches Landhaus (Herrengasse 13). Not only did the Academy lack sufficient rooms for scientific activities, it also had no facilities for festive occasions. It has to be mentioned at this point that the university was one of the centres of the dramatic events of the 1848 revolution: On 12 May 1848 students gathered at the university and demanded a radical reorganisation of the political system. This event has been recorded in a painting by Franz Schams (1823–1883), showing the students' guardroom in the aula of the University of Vienna (**Fig. 51**). On 25 May the government decreed that the university be closed.

In the search for proper accommodation for the Academy interest began to focus on the university building. On the basis of a note of 30 July 1855 to the Minister of Finance, Freiherr Karl Ludwig von Bruck, the Academy finally moved into the former university building in 1857, 10 years after its foundation, and has stayed there ever since. The Minister of Education, Leo Graf Thun, at that time referred to the plans for the establishment of an academy during the reign of Maria Theresa, which had never been implemented. He wrote:: "[...] If the building in question, originally dedicated to the arts and sciences (Artibus et Scientiis), is now assigned to be used by the Academy of Sciences, this use seems to be even more appropriate as Maria Theresa had already committed herself to the establishment of an Academy of Sciences and had, indeed, even taken a decision to that effect. [...]". He thus underlined that the two most ambitious projects, the construction of a new university and the plans to establish an Imperial Academy of Sciences, have their roots in Maria Theresa's era.

At the end of 1856 the military administration that had occupied the building in the wake of the revolution finally moved out and the building was handed over to the Academy on 3 January 1857. The substantial restoration and adaptation costs were borne by the government, and from 1859 onwards the Academy received an annual budget for its maintenance. At the official transfer ceremony on 29 October 1857 the Minister of the Interior Alexander Freiherr von Bach proudly stated: "[...] The Imperial Academy of Sciences, an association of gentlemen entrusted with the great and beneficial task to promote the sciences through independent research as well as by supporting and encouraging others to do so in the interest of human society and our beloved fatherland, is now moving into the halls of this magnificent building and making it its permanent home.

[...] In fact, the legacy of our immortal Empress could not have received a better dedication than being assigned to the Academy. [...]".

The first scientific activities of the Academy

In the first stage, after the dramatic situation of the 1848 revolution had calmed down, the scientific activities in the field of humanities concentrated on source editions (medieval documents and works of the church fathers), research into the Romance languages, philosophy and jurisprudence. In the natural sciences the institution initially focused mainly on meteorology and geology as well as on research in the fields of botany, medicine and zoology. In the years 1879 to 1897, when it was headed by the prominent historian Alfred Ritter von Arneth (1819–1897), the Academy developed into a universal research institution, and between 1897 and 1914 its position was further strengthened and enhanced by the cooperation with similar institutions on an international level. During the First World War the Academy did its best to continue its activities, the war, however, affected in particular its expeditions to the Near East.

The Academy in the First Republic

After the end of the First World War the statutes of the Academy had to be adapted to the new situation. It was renamed "Academy of Sciences in Vienna". Studies now concentrated on philology and history and the mathematical-natural sciences section was particular successful in areas such as the geomagnetism and ethnography, morphology and anthropology. One of the members of the mathematical-natural sciences section, the famous physicist Erwin Schrödinger, was even awarded the Nobel Prize for his contribution to quantum mechanics in 1933. In 1934 the Academy started to hold public lectures and thus opened the door to the sciences for the general public. This tradition has been continued to this day. At the same time efforts were made to establish international contacts and to intensify the networking of research projects.

The Academy during the "Third Reich"

The "Anschluss", the annexation of Austria to the Third Reich, in March 1938 severely affected the Academy, which had now become member of the "Association of German Academies of the Reich". A major shake-up took place in the leading positions and the historian Heinrich (Ritter von) Srbik

(1878–1951), a major exponent of a Pan-German conception of history, was appointed President. All the Jewish members and many others were expelled from the Academy. Even though the name "Austria" was deleted from the map by the regime, the Academy continued to work on its traditional publications "Archives for Austrian History" and "Fontes rerum Austriacarum" under their old names. The position of the Academy between 1938 and 1945 might be described as somewhere between adaptation and resistance: In many areas it conformed with the wishes of the new regime, while it offered considerable resistance to any restriction of its scope of action. Among other things it succeeded in retaining its right to have potential new members nominated by the ordinary members – against proposals made by the regime or the Reichsdozentenführung. In 1941 Srbik achieved the release of the famous Dutch historian Johan Huizinga, a corresponding member of the Academy, from a detention camp.

The Academy after 1945

After the end of the war and the collapse of the National Socialist regime in 1945 the Federal Law governing the standing and activities of the Academy of 14 October 1921 (as amended in 1925) was reinstated. The "interim statutes" passed in 1938 were rescinded and the functions of the Presidium declared to have come to an end. On 18 May 1945 thirteen Academy members then present in Vienna gathered at the building of the Vienna University to hold a first "General Meeting". As the Academy building had been damaged in the war, further General Meetings of the Academy took place, until October 1945, at the Seminar of Philology of the University of Vienna. On 31 October 1945 a solemn meeting was held in the "Auditorium maximum" of Vienna University. Ernst Späth was elected interim head of the Academy and Richard Meister (1881–1964) became his deputy. Ordinary and corresponding members of the Academy resident in Austria who were identified as members of National Socialist institutions (both those who had joined NS institutions at the time when the NS party was illegal. i.e. before 1938, and those who had joined during the NS regime) were professionally disqualified and relegated from the Academy in line with Austrian anti-Nazi legislation.

A decision of major importance was the change of the name of the institution: The "Academy of Sciences in Vienna", as it had been called since 1921, was renamed "Austrian Academy of Sciences" in order to emphasise its significance for the whole of Austria, which is reflected, amongst other things, by the fact that research institutions of the Academy are currently found in seven of the nine Austrian provinces.

After the first lean years of the post-war period, the years from 1947 to 1966 saw the Academy not only develop along traditional lines but also break new ground in both domestic and international research activities, preparing the soil for the inclusion of new areas of research and the founding of many new institutions in response to recent developments in the world of the arts and sciences.

Milestones in mathematical and scientific research were the establishment of the Institute of Molecular Biology on 1 January 1966 and the Institute of High-Energy Physics on 1 April of the same year, which helped the Academy to catch up with leading European centres. In the same year, the Academy took over the Wilhelminenberg Research Station (today the Konrad Lorenz Institute for Comparative Ethology). In 1971, it founded the Erich Schmid Institute of Solid State Physics (today the Erich Schmid Institute of Materials Science) at Leoben, in 1972 the Institutes of Information Processing (Vienna), Limnology (Mondsee) and Space Research (Graz). These were followed in 1974 by the Institute of Biophysics and X-Ray Structure Research in Graz (today the Institute of Biophysics and Nanosystems Research) and in 1987 by the Institute of Medium Energy Physics (today the Stefan Meyer Institute of Subatomic Physics) in Vienna. The first Academy research institution to be founded in the western part of Austria was the Institute of Biomedical Aging Research established at Innsbruck in 1991. In 1994 this was followed by the founding of the Institute for Technology Assessment in Vienna.

The year 2003 saw the establishment of the Johann Radon Institute for Computational and Applied Mathematics in Linz and the Institute for Quantum Optics and Quantum Information located in Innsbruck and Vienna, 2004 the foundation of the Research Unit for Integrated Sensor Systems at Wiener Neustadt and 2006 the Research Units for Respiratory Gas Analysis at Dornbirn and for Geographic Information Science at Salzburg.

Organisationally, the Academy broke new ground by founding three research units in the form of limited liability companies, the Institute of Molecular Biotechnology GmbH (IMBA), the Gregor Mendel Institute of Molecular Plant Biology GmbH (GMI) and the Research Centre for Molecular Medicine GmbH (CeMM). The former two institutes are accommodated in the "ÖAW – Life Sciences Centre Vienna" (Dr. Bohrgasse, Vienna III.) opened in May 2006 (**Fig. 52**), while the CeMM will have its home in a newly erected building in the AKH (General Hospital) complex. This rounds off the Academy's major building projects, which also included the construction of a research building in Graz in the year 2000.

As regards the programme of the philosophic-historical section, mention should first and foremost be made of the major research projects in the fields of history and philology undertaken by the "Commission for Editing the Corpus of the Latin Church Fathers (CSEL)", the "Historical Commission" (founded as early as 1847) and the "Commission for the Publication of the Diplomata Volume (Vienna Edition)" (founded in 1875) and, along with these activities, of a wealth of research projects and publications on a variety of subjects: medieval writings and printed publications, archaeology, literary forms, theatre studies, history of art, cultural studies, medieval realia, biographies of Austrian personalities, urban and regional research and demography. Focal points of research were defined by the establishment of a number of new institutes from the mid-1960s onwards. In 1967, the Institute for the Study of Medieval Realia (now Institute for the Study of Realia of the Middle Ages and Early Modern Era) was founded at Krems, followed in 1975 by the Vienna Institute of Demography, in 1992 by the Vienna Institute for the Cultural and Intellectual History of Asia, and in 2002 the Vienna Institute of Iranian Studies, the successor to a long-standing Academy commission devoted to this subject.

With its wide variety of methodologically diverse research projects, the Austrian Academy of Sciences is currently Austria's largest and most important extra-universitarian fundamental research institution.

"ÖAW – LIFE SCIENCES ZENTRUM WIEN" (DR. BOHRGASSE, WIEN III.) (FIG. 52)

Annex: Source materials

Plans

Vienna, Albertina, AZ allgemein, Mappe 45, Umschlag 5: 12/8028, 13/8029, 14/8030, 15/8031 (set of four ground plans: basement, ground floor, main and second storey). Umschlag 6: 18/8026, 16/8023, 17/8024, 17a/8025 (set of four ground plans: ground floor, main storey, two plans of second storey); Umschlag 7: 19/8027 (elevation Observatory)

Vienna, Akademie der bildenden Künste, Kupferstichkabinett, Inv.-No. 16718, 16783, 16784, 16785 (set of four plans; façade elevation, ground plan of ground floor, longitudinal section, longitudinal elevation)

Vienna, Wien Museum, Inv.-No. 114.810 (pen drawing with watercolour wash, 1754/1755, Gregorio Guglielmi's sketch for Great Hall ceiling)

Archival documents

Vienna, Österreichisches Staatsarchiv, Allgemeines Verwaltungsarchiv, Studienhofkommission, Karton 7, Sign. 4, Akt 12 ex 1753, fol. 5r–9v (Cost estimate of the "Directorium in publicis et cameralibus" for Maria Theresa of 26 February 1753), Akt 13 ex 1753, fol. 17r–23r (Submission of the "Directorium in publicis et cameralibus" to Maria Theresa of 15 March 1753)

Vienna, Österreichisches Staatsarchiv, Haus-, Hof- und Staatsarchiv, Hofbauamt, Karton 2 (1761–1770), Umschlag 2, fol. 28r-30r (Cost estimates for repairs of the University building, 1764/1765)

Wien, Österreichische Akademie der Wissenschaften, Archiv, Karton 186 and 187 (Conversions and adaptations of the building between ca. 1856 and 1939, some of later date)

Further references are contained in the publications of Justus Schmidt and Renate Wagner-Rieger. However, verification is impossible on account of the frequent absence of archival details.

Bibliography (in chronological order)

Scheyb, Franz Christoph, Musae Francisco et Mariae Theresiae Augustis congratulantur ob scientias bonasque artes eorum iussu et munificentia Vindobonae restitutas, Vienna 1756

Scheyb, Franz Christoph, Heinrich Jasomirgott, eine Lobschrift auf Ihre Kaiserliche und Koenigliche Majestaeten bey Gelegenheit der uralten Universität zu Wien von dem Arkader Orestrio, Vienna 1756

Maister SJ, Georgius, Panegyricus Francisco et Mariae Theresiae Augustis ob scientias optimasque artes suis in terris instauratas, ornatas, (...), Vienna 1756 (published also in French)

Colland, Friedrich, Kurzer Inbegriff von dem Ursprunge der Wissenschaften, Schulen, Akademien, und Universitaeten in ganz Europa, besonders aber der Akademien und hohen Schulen zu Wien (...), Vienna 1796

Luca, Ignaz de, Neuester wienerischer Wegweiser für Fremde und Inländer vom Jahr 1797. Oder kurze Beschreibung aller Merkwürdigkeiten Wiens, Vienna 1797

Wolf, Ferdinand Joseph, Über wissenschaftliche Akademien mit besonderer Beziehung auf die k. oesterreichische, Vienna 1856

Weinkopf, Anton, Beschreibung der k.k. Akademie der Bildenden Künste in Wien, Vienna 1875

Lützow, Carl von, Geschichte der kais. kön. Akademie der Bildenden Künste. Festschrift zur Eröffnung des neuen Akademie-Gebäudes, Vienna 1877

Arneth, Alfred Ritter von, Die Wiener Universität unter Maria Theresia, Vienna 1879

Karajan, Theodor Georg von, Address on the occasion of the transfer of the former university building to the Imperial Academy of Sciences, delivered on 29 October 1857, Vienna 1897

Schmidt, Justus, Die alte Universität in Wien und ihr Erbauer Jean Nicolas Jadot. Preface by Julius Schlosser (Wiener Forschungen zur Kunstgeschichte), Vienna–Leipzig 1929

Meister, Richard, Geschichte der Akademie der Wissenschaften in Wien 1847–1947 (Österreichische Akademie der Wissenschaften, Denkschriften der Gesamtakademie 1), Vienna 1947

Gall, Franz, Die Alte Universität (Wiener Geschichtsbücher 1), Vienna–Hamburg 1970

Wagner-Rieger, Renate, Das Haus der Akademie der Wissenschaften. Commemorative gift on the occasion of the 125th anniversary of the Academy, Vienna 1972

Antonicek, Theophil, Musik im Festsaal der Österreichischen Akademie der Wissenschaften (Österreichische Akademie der Wissenschaften, Sitzungsberichte der phil.-hist. Klasse 277), Vienna 1972

Hamann, Günther / Mühlberger, Kurt / Skacel, Franz (Eds.), Das alte Universitätsviertel in Wien, 1385–1985 (Schriftenreihe des Universitätsarchivs 2), Vienna 1985

Garms, Jörg, Jadot und Italien: zwischen Lothringen und Wien, in: Römische Historische Mitteilungen 31 (1989), 319–338

"Viertel mit Vergangenheit ... und Zukunft". Public lectures of the Austrian Academy of Sciences 1987, Vienna 1990

Hittmair, Otto / Hunger, Herbert (Eds.), Akademie der Wissenschaften. Entwicklung einer österreichischen Forschungsinstitution (Österreichische Akademie der Wissenschaften, Denkschriften der Gesamtakademie XV), Vienna 1997

Garms, Jörg, Jean Nicolas Jadot, in: Contini, Alessandra / Parri, Maria Grazia (Eds.), Il Granducato di Toscana e i Lorena nel secolo XVIII. Kongreßakten (Florence 1994), Florence 1999, 417–426

Lorenz, Hellmut (Ed.), Barock (Geschichte der Bildenden Kunst in Österreich 4), Munich–London–New York 1999, 298–299, nr. 66 (Huberta Weigl)

Garms, Jörg, Der Architekt Jean Nicolas Jadot (1710–1761), in: Renate Zedinger (Ed.), Lothringens Erbe, Franz Stephen von Lothringen (1708–1765) und sein Wirken in Wirtschaft, Wissenschaft und Kunst in der Habsburgermonarchie. Exhibition catalogue Schallaburg, St. Pölten 2000, 211–222

Telesko, Werner, Das Programm des Deckenfreskos im Festsaal des Hauptgebäudes der Österreichischen Akademie der Wissenschaften in Wien, in: Hilscher, Elisabeth Theresia / Sommer-Mathis, Andrea (Eds.), Pietro Metastasio – uomo universale (1698–1782). Commemorative gift of the Austrian Academy of Sciences on the occasion of the 300th anniversary of Pietro Metastasio (Österreichische Akademie der Wissenschaften, Sitzungsberichte der phil.-hist. Klasse 676), Vienna 2000, 355–365

Langen, Stefanie von, Vier wenig beachtete Deckenentwürfe von Gregorio Guglielmi, in: Barockberichte 2000, H. 28, 612–623

Csáky, Moritz, Altes Universitätsviertel: Erinnerungsraum, Gedächtnisort, in: Csáky, Moritz / Stachel, Peter (Eds.), Die Verortung von Gedächtnis (Zweiter Internationaler Kongreß des Forschungsprogramms "Orte des Gedächtnisses"), Vienna 2001, 257–277

Telesko, Werner, Kunsthistorische Bemerkungen zum "alten Universitätsviertel" in Wien als "Gedächtnisort", in: Csáky, Moritz / Stachel, Peter (Eds.), Die Verortung von Gedächtnis (Zweiter Internationaler Kongreß des Forschungsprogramms "Orte des Gedächtnisses"), Vienna 2001, 279–302

Flyer "Österreichische Akademie der Wissenschaften", Text by Hermann Fillitz, Vienna 2002

Karner, Herbert / Telesko, Werner (Eds.), Die Jesuiten in Wien. Zur Kunst- und Kulturgeschichte der österreichischen Ordensprovinz der "Gesellschaft Jesu" im 17. und 18. Jahrhundert (Veröffentlichungen der Kommission für Kunstgeschichte der Österreichischen Akademie der Wissenschaften 5), Vienna 2003

Karner, Herbert, Wien – vom Jesuiterplatzl zum Universitätsplatz, in: Jahrbuch der Österreichischen Gesellschaft zur Erforschung des 18. Jahrhunderts 18/19 (2004), 397–412, 569–575 (Figs.)

Feichtinger, Johannes / Uhl, Heidemarie, Die Österreichische Akademie der Wissenschaften nach 1945. Eine Gelehrtengesellschaft im Spannungsfeld von Wissenschaft, Politik und Gesellschaft, in: Grandner, Margarete / Heiss, Gernot / Rathkolb, Oliver (Eds.), Zukunft mit Altlasten. Die Universität Wien 1945 bis 1955 (Querschnitte 19), Innsbruck-Vienna-Munich-Bolzano 2005, 313–337

Hedwig Kopetz, Die Österreichische Akademie der Wissenschaften. Aufgaben, Rechtstellung, Organisation (Studien zur Politik und Verwaltung 88), Vienna 2006

Telesko, Werner, Das Programm der Deckenmalereien im Johannessaal der alten Wiener Universität – katholische Aufklärung versus barocke Allegorik, in: Csáky, Moritz / Celestini, Federico / Tragatschnig, Ulrich (Eds.), Barock – ein Ort des Gedächtnisses. Interpretament der Moderne / Postmoderne, Vienna–Cologne–Weimar 2007, 17–37

Illustration credits

Vienna, ÖAW: 1–3, 20 (Sammlung Woldan); 4, 21, 34, 37, 39, 52

Vienna, ÖAW, Kommission für Kunstgeschichte: 5

Vienna, Karl Pani: 10, 11, 13, 16, 17, 21–33, 37, 40–43, 45–47, 49, 50

Prague, Czech Academy of Sciences, Institute of the History of Art (Martin Mádl): 6

Vienna, Kunsthistorisches Museum: 7

Vienna, Akademie der bildenden Künste, Kupferstichkabinett: 9, 18, 19

Vienna, Albertina: 12, 14, 15

Vienna, Österreichische Nationalbibliothek, Bildarchiv: 8, 35, 36, 44, 51

Vienna, Wien Museum: 38

Vienna, Belvedere: 48